Black Laurel

Black Laurel

Poems

Michele Poulos

Iris Press
Oak Ridge, Tennessee

Cover painting ("A Part of It") Copyright © 2012 by Lorella Paleni

Design by Robert B. Cumming, Jr.

Library of Congress Cataloging-in-Publication Data

Names: Poulos, Michele, 1970 author.
Title: Black laurel : poems / Michele Poulos.
Description: Oak Ridge, Tennessee : Iris Press, 2016.
Identifiers: LCCN 2016002967 | ISBN 9781604542356 (pbk. : alk. paper)
Classification: LCC PS3616.O8568 A6 2016 | DDC 811/.6—dc23
LC record available at http://lccn.loc.gov/2016002967

Acknowledgments

Grateful acknowledgment is made to the editors of the following magazines in which these poems first appeared, sometimes in slightly different versions:

Connotation Press: An Online Artifact: "Augury," "Letter to Titos Patrikios," "Letter to Tryfon Tolides," "Apology in Red," and "New Husband"

Hinchas de Poesía: "Thread & Drone," "Clematis," and "Retrograde to Desire"

The Hollins Critic: "The Angel of Broken Instruments"

Illuminations: "Letter to the Egyptian Fishmonger," and "Requiem Wind"

MiPOesias: "Rilke's Eighth Letter"

Miracle Monocle: "Devotion"

Smartish Pace: "Letter to Gregory with Haymow's Gold"

The Southern Review: "The Golden Age of Herbalists"

Sycamore Review: "*Ausschusskinder:* the garbage children"

Waccamaw: "End of Blood Orange Blossoms"

"Thursdays in the Faubourg Marigny" was chosen by Matthew Dickman for inclusion in *Best New Poets 2012.*

"Letter to Gregory with Haymow's Gold" was a finalist for the 2012 Beullah Rose Poetry Prize by *Smartish Pace.*

Some of these poems appeared in the chapbook *A Disturbance in the Air,* winner of the 2012 Slapering Hol Press Chapbook Competition.

Special thanks to all those who read my work and offered such helpful advice, especially my teachers at Arizona State University, Norman Dubie, T.R. Hummer, Cynthia Hogue, and Beckian Fritz-Goldberg, and at Virginia Commonwealth University, David Wojahn and Kathleen Graber. Thanks to my fellow poets and writers for their insightful comments and beneficial critiques: Margo Taft Stever, B.K. Fischer, Peggy Ellsberg, Jennifer Franklin, Sara Sams, Rachel Andoga, Dexter Booth, Eman Hassan, John-Michael Bloomquist, Sarah Grieve, Spencer Hanvick, Christine Holm, Catherine Murray, Scott Montgomery, Nathan Slinker, Reese Conner, Lauren Espinoza, Kitt Keller, Kathleen Winter, and Chris Miller.

Grateful acknowledgment is owed to Arizona State University's creative writing program and the Virginia G. Piper Center for Creative Writing for their fellowships, which allowed invaluable time to begin this book. Immense gratitude is due to my family and friends for their ongoing support without which this book might not have been written, especially Mary Ann, Megan, and Max Cisne. I also wish to thank Anna Journey and David St. John for their guidance, and Gregory Donovan for his unwavering enthusiasm.

I am deeply grateful to Robert and Beto Cumming of Iris Press for giving this manuscript a home.

for Greg

light to the harbor

Contents

ONE

TWO

THREE

Someone, I tell you, in another time,
remembers us.

—Sappho, *Fragment 147*

ONE

The White Rabbit

beside the house with emerald trim

is large and heavy as a sack of flour,
ears rimmed with dark brown fur.

It sits so terribly still

the possibility presents itself
the animal is stuffed.

I search its face for the slightest motion,
search its body for injury.
When I draw within arm's reach,

I bend to meet it, eye-level,
where its whiskers shake
in the acacia-scented breeze.

Its eyes lock on my own, and for a moment
I see its histories
in the dark bands there: the birth

beneath the sweet olive,
the child carrying it home in her arms
where she offers it milk,
the makeshift cage in the garage,
the day it escapes, the long nights after,

and now this: a blank plea
that the uncertainty of its life be finished.

Wouldn't I have come sooner to keep you
from harm?

Let me take you back through the fields,

       you who never turned from me,
    who held violets in your mouth.

New Husband

He has done
all he can: emptied half
the closet, moved his razor
to another shelf.
He's hidden the photos
of the first wife in the attic
beside the fishing rod
and the box of lures
in their lichen
of seawater patina.
He's done everything
he knows to do.

Still, he'll hear the hours
through the floorboards,
the ache that will marry
and marry him
to my old city: the diner
with its brick walls, dog
statue in the cemetery,
the man who once summoned
me with his warm hand.
At night the woods twill
the clapboard siding.
Such long winter months.
All the owls starving.

Letter to Titos Patrikios

And the echo that was sent out of the past
all of us heard and knew
          —Odysseus Elytis

If, standing before a band of soldiers, the open

mouths of their guns infinite as night, you have seen

the Gate of Athena Archegetis surrender its marble

to the sky, who can blame you for believing?

At sixteen, you understand beauty as the ruin

a city can no longer witness and as the heat

the bodies in your home will radiate. Once,

your mother's blouse, dusted with cinnamon

and clove, burned against your skin

red with fever. Cities are like this: they offer

us the world before they finally let go.

The fog in the harbor knows this, perhaps

has known it all along, yet returns—as if not

returning would mean there could be nothing

left to see. Here you are, trembling

at the western gate of the agora; a soldier's

cough sharpens your hearing. You won't cry.

To cry is to erase a fallen whitewashed

stair. If you must gaze unflinchingly

down the well of a gun, you'll do it.

We hear the shot ring out, if only

in your dream. Titos, let me tell you a secret.

The dead don't care if the wind is absent

from the mountain or if the sea holds yet another

bronze head. The world is softly breaking.

We know your story: a girl rode up

on a bicycle, stopped the bullets in their casings.

You came to believe then in the wonder

of a peach dress, which is the same belief

that now allows your feet a dip in the surf.

A boy will do everything he can for his country.

The whole landscape breathing every day,

hard as it can.

Unmanned

I no longer love blue skies.
        —*Zubair Rehman, congressional testimony*

That wolf-belly gray—a new belief.
        [And clouds]

        [And knots of rain]

Grandmother who once picked okra outside her back door.

                Grandmother bent over yellow petals, drones

                buzzing an open box of sky.

You might find yourself

        beneath a bruised horizon,

another dark belief threading

                its injury through a field in Pakistan.

                Not a white-eyed buzzard. Not a desert lark.

Glass eye cruising the wind.

                UAVs have everything to do
                        with the terror of wings flapping.

What prayer might hasten a fog

        thick as a bear skull?

[Shared blanket under leaves]

[Village song beyond the hill]

When the machines come,

souls, like chaff, will fly.

Thread & Drone

i.

At dusk in the burn of rush-
   lights
  on the hillside,

a dirge howls

  in the woman's mouth,

   a keening song

   old
  as Andromache's
    lament.

  It begins with a drone
tunneling the body

   with flame,
bees stirring
  the chest. The fluid

  drift of its thread

feathers
   the interior.

The pitch breezes
    the dead

  through olive leaves,

   rises the way

oblivious stars
       rise:

    an infinitesimal scuttle
whose sweep
    is unchanging.

Each sigh disturbs

    the air

      a little more

as if to say *what rapture,*

what sea returns
    its forever to our ears.

ii.

    Where a coin
is held in the cold hand

& a clutch of hair ripped

    from the skull
& flung on the coffin,

    these twilight gestures

give us Greece. *O cypress tree!*

O arch and pillar!

When she fades,
    the next voice

embroiders the song

with guests & ceremonies,

even the tools
of the dead one's
profession

will appear.

If he was a mason,
his trowel weeps

tears of lime & ash.

If a shepherd,

the goats & ewes refuse
the fields that hold them

& march single file

into the sea.

iii.

When dirt is finally thrown
over the coffin,

a mourner's cry soars
into a storm

groaning through walls

until her hair uncoils
& with her nails

she slashes

her cheeks.

An infininte

knot of black-clad women
surrounds her,

their clasped hands strung

like pearls

against the wind

that hurries their feet.

Apology in Red

If every day I am forgotten a little more,
      driving home beneath the cloak
of desert mountain when the heat

           lays down a stilled hand over the valley,
      I am reminded again how sadness accumulates

in the shuffle of red dust
      beading the summer, as if each thing
           were too intensely itself, needing to soften.

And when the earth turns red, it seems
      it's always been this way, a loose powder
dusted over surfaces familiar as the stair

           before a front door. Red in the attic, red clinging
      to toaster and book spines, red nesting
           in my lungs. There is a peace in having it

everywhere, and I begin to forget
      how I once lived and fall into this new hushed
           swath of color that ends

      as all things must
           beyond the sliver of sight.

My friend's mother died only yesterday, I see her
      staring
at what was always there flickering in the corner

           until the dim bud in her eyes faded. A last breath,
      he said, so strong it could have sucked
           leaves from the gutters. And if you had a choice,

wouldn't you, too, have your last breath
    drink the creosote from night?

    A woman once asked for my spiritual color. *Green,*
I said, recalling my childhood room,

    walls painted with that secret
in new grass, and in its bright unfolding I was taught

how to be at home outdoors,
    to take in steadiness from the timpani
of rain, and from the yellow heart

    of a willow, kindness.
        And her answer? *Red,*
she said, *because it is impenetrable.*

    And if you ask me right now,
    I would say it's easy to mistake
regret for the ash beneath this hard pan
    that longs for a strict rain to release it.

    And what would the rain do anyway
but pound craters into craters in the dust.

Either way, it will come.
    We'll take from it what we can.

Requiem Wind

Statues at night recall
                    the pale winter,

whisper scenes of my first house—
              the one that burned

when I was seven. Sometimes they speak
      of flames high as pines
           or needles scattered across the patio,
           turnips blackened in a crate—

other times, it is my mother's hands
folding with the nettles of the sun.

Every room the soldiers burned that year
                      was a way of saying

          we moved from town to town.
    Though I don't know everything about houses,

I can feel their daydreams and phantoms
      sometimes, when I stand still;

    At times—

          near the water, in rooms stripped bare
of linen, rotted pears in a bowl,

                waves subtracting the shore
as if no future clemency were possible—

        I remember and I cannot sleep.

History is a blue pomegranate
     split in the open grass filling you with simplehearted stars

    and cold rot.

                Though I couldn't say now
if the shutters were yellow or white,

     the hills keep on emptying,
              giving themselves over.

Don't talk to me about the warbler,

     or the tawny-colored lark.

    Their souls too are restless,
         shifting from window to window—

lifetimes spent mistaking a flash
    in the harbor for what could not fly away.

Don't talk about the little wagtail
     tracing figures with his long feathers on the light.

       Which is to say:
         there is no warm quay
         that would draw me.

Some nights become
     a statue's cool finger on my throat:

    the moon's white rag
dissolves into the wretched
    awareness of a child:

a fetid city decays
to burgeon over and over again—

though sometimes a breeze carries
the shape of a young face from the village,

a baker or dressmaker
with lips pink as a sheep's tongue.

If only houses could remember the skies
that astonished and the children

beneath them whose delicate fingers counted,
on each hand, the dead

before finally turning over,
quietly beneath a blanket,

changeless

as the marble stair.

Letter to Gregory with Haymow's Gold

A sycamore climbs through the silo
like a spine, twin-hearted seeds whistling
to the ground as the barn squats beside it

in its injured neglect. The tree won't remember
any of this,

not the curved wall pressing it into shape,
nor the bees carrying white millet
through the wind,

lulling the meadow
into a completion
that drifts back to your childhood,

the driveway edged with walnut trees,
the farmhouse not yet undressed
of its linen. Your grandfather

in his dusty hat swinging a bucket
of milk by his side.

What you knew of the soul was the watery stillness
of a calf's eye whose center drew you
into your own deepening.

Nights you would tuck yourself into the haymow's gold,
believing in the divinity of land's open hand,

how each blade of grass shrugged off the dew
to become wholly itself again, & give yourself fully

to the only god that would ever have you.

Now, there comes a point
           when a man strains to remember
     what he used to believe:

the motes, flickering,
          held up to the light through a barn door.

Before his cousins inherited the land

                & argued about the worth of a walnut tree,

before cattle sold to the highest bidder.

The question persists:

          will the field remember the trees it once held

             & the animals whose silhouettes at dusk
          underscored the night's vastness?

Nothing stands
between us and the summer,

          having grown quiet,
             having given over.

When the Wind Falls

—Korifi Voiou, Greece

I.

Moments after the exposed film begins
its long fade, the boy runs away
to carve the date with a stick
in the dirt, *April 6, 1941,* while his sister
lays out the walls of a bedroom
in crocus blossoms curling in the sun.
At home, in the summer kitchen's cool,
their mother pounds dough into bread.
Deep in her own dream, the girl presses
two cornhusk dolls together shy of a kiss
in the seconds before she hears,

                   at first, a distant
roar, perhaps a neighbor's tractor
ploughing or a growl hidden in the woods.
Soon it grows thin as a falcon's call
sailing its broad-winged shadow across the field
and she is amused.

                  It must be her brother,
she thinks, eyes shifting toward the boy.
Earlier, he had lifted a kite made of silk
into the air, the tail curling between limbs
tracing sky. His hand pauses now
in midair, as though pointing toward a star.
He laughs, uncertain why the wind

                   roils like gunfire at his back.

2.

Seventy years on, that same wind kicks
up the dust in Syntagma Square to blind
the demonstrators and photographers who will
fascinate the world with the idea that all of Greece
is burning. And if I refuse to point a finger,
it is that such fears are useless
as a cracked baseball bat
                      kept under a bed
or shutters fastened against the night's slow shuffle.
Neighbors here are feared.
First the Turks, then the Germans,
now Albanians. Though the Nazis
have disappeared, brothers and sisters are still locked
in rivalry over homes once occupied.
Rooms that were once fragrant with the scent
of rose liquor and golden plums, *tiropita* baking
in the oven,
                    are now mute
as the spooked black-and-white photos
trapped behind glass at the heads of graves—
there the relatives lay, one body piled
on top of another, to be dug up seven years on,
bones washed, spread in the field to burn dry
before being squeezed into a warehoused shoebox.
                  But the dead have a knack
for returning.

3.

And if I'm feeling sad here now, it's that
the church with the turquoise dome overlooking
the meadow where the children played
has sealed itself, the incense burner gone cool
as the plaster wall where Saint Demetrius hangs,
the blade of his spear buried inside his foe's chest.
One day a stranger will come to the village
                    dressed as a nun,
stuff his pockets with change
from the poor box, then leave
his costume draped over a low-hanging
olive branch, frightening a group
of children on their way home from school.
Their screams will fade into fields
and dust, quick as my aunt's scream,
                    that girl of 1941,
terrified by the round belly of the plane, the spray
of bullets that shattered the spell around her.
And if I'm bewildered, it's because nothing
will ever be as sure as the thick black cross
under each wing shrouding her
                    like night's ragged shawl.

Utterance

Still bound to dream, my lover's breath
is a highballing train the bridge can hardly
hold, quick as his brother's slip
from a church roof, three-story fall
to white earth, ten years coupled
to a wheelchair until he blew the hole
through his mind's eye.

Think of my lover mopping up
bloodied linoleum, splintered bone.
A family lapsed into freighted absence.
In the dream, he makes love to a woman.
He means to say, *You are the temple-eye
of my passage*, but mumbles instead, *We, too,
are untongued in the star-field of smoke.*

Thursdays in the Faubourg Marigny

Midnights, I'd slink from the house,
done up for Vaughan's Lounge,
that piece of down-home-dirty,
swagger through New Orleans avenues
thick with Mississippi steam,
black slip dress slit up the side, black
tights battered with snags, powdered,
baked, glittered, the night
holding its soft wrists open.
Easy as the club's silver notes sliding
over the sidewalk and through barbeque
smoke, meat cooked out of the back
of a pickup truck, tin foil glinting
like the teeth of that man in the alley.
I fed him his hot sauce, thumbprint of red
whorled on each nipple, hips peaked
like bald cypress knees, his mouth
pulling at my breast as though refusing
isolation, as if I could lay bare
each burrowed place inside him, the sucking
at first hard, then pleading and reckless
as the staggered walk back to his place,
where for hours we fucked in full dark
broken by the cheap blue neon
wailing across the street, a sign whose light
scattered over the skeleton mask
he'd slipped on: bulbous forehead,
grid of teeth, eyes hollow as a gouge
of earth, nose an upside-down heart.
It was Death come knocking,
night-winged and thieving, and all I gave
was stars kindled, body flown.

TWO

TWO

The Angel of Broken Instruments

These wings are not muslin,
ermine-colored, or petal-light,
but stitched with red and black felt
and pulled tight across the bones
of tubas and trombones; they coil
over my thin shoulders.
I might appear anywhere. Called
to the side of a man chain-smoking
on his way home after an argument
with his son, we are stopped short
on the corner of Third and Main
by a piano fallen from the sky.

He has mistaken the heap for an old love
as he kneels beside the splintered maple
to gather the steel wires and wood
into a nest he carries in his arms
to the river, where he sets it afloat
on the stream. We are always more
than what we believe.
                    As a bad child
I was banished to the basement,
where for hours I'd spin myself
on a stool with clawed feet clutching
three amber glass spheres, the harp tinkling
each time a moth grazed its strings.
Though I couldn't play, I imagined
a song so electric that the air
parted for its passage,
where notes multiplied and divided,
and once it finished, the wind
was no longer disordered.

When I found the wrecked piano
left in the field, I curled up inside it
while the bearded wheat grew tall
and noiseless.

Textures of the Cave

I.

Female genitalia charcoaled on a stalactite—
       doorway to the spirit world.
       32,000 years pass as an instant.

Fresh as yesterday, the line dividing
       thigh from thigh ends at the bottom
       of the cone, while the top half

of the figure, partially obscured,
       blurs into the head of a bison.
       Among the paintings on these cave walls,

only this one depicts a human form.
       Some say that's to be expected:
       the artists were men, and young.

Others say shamans charmed power from walls,
       painting their visions into images made
       with iron oxide and animal fat, chuffing

powder through reeds onto rock
       smeared with sap and grease. Some beasts
       are drawn one directly over another,

maybe thousands of years apart,
       the theory being: once the animal was killed,
       the power of the image was exhausted.

They were forced to begin again.

2.

The body's betrayal always a blaze of pain:
                my lover's hand a stranger's
           after three months apart,

                    for now the touch
disintegrates…

   The customary whisper—

a scene from a film

                    or another life—

*   a eunuch unfastens me*
for the sultan, on his hands

*   a vintage scent of mint*
*   & damask rose in this mute assembly.*

*   Each night unsheeted*
for the bath tiered with marble
*   thick as the wrist that dips*
*   beneath its surface,*

*   the fountain's terraced cascade*
*   like stifled pleasure*
*   torn over & over*
*   from the body.*

*   Each tiled tulip*
along the courtyard a nod
*   to the Golden Horn. I am nothing*

*   more than instrument*
in these tented hallways,

a slumber of oiled curves
        led when clean by the arm
to the one on the throne.

And when the candle's tail falters?
        And when the last of the soiled water drains?

My heart vacant as dusk where the dark
            corners of a chamber bend inward
    into its effaced center
        until even shame burns out—

At what point will we dissolve

                or remain in the story?

3.

A friend, in his priestly way, sweeps
blue eagle feathers along my body,
a blessing while sage burns
to sweeten the air. He rubs red clay
from *the mother cave* of the Hopi
into my skin, guiding me into visualization:
begin with a rose-colored light
at your tailbone, & below your navel,
amber, & at your brow, a violet light
with pink at the edges spilling away… lean
into the colors—they are, like you, inevitable.

4.

After hours of thirst, the body's feral

atoms spin uncertain as the measurement

of scientists who descend into the opening

of Chauvet and yet still cannot determine how

much time passed between a boy's shallow footprint

& the paw print of a wolf laid down beside it.

Waists cinched with ropes, lights swinging

through that dark, we know ourselves there

as intruders, as if to trespass that deep

into the earth is apology, as if a bird

found flying through its walls had lost

its trust in the sky, & the bear's skull,

glassed in calcite, must defy all our explanation.

5.

Down here,
the world

no longer presses
too hard

upon me—
if there are

shadows,
they descend

from a vastness
of sky from

which I turn
away. Black

iris. Black bough
I mistake

for the silk
of an antler.

I am trying
to grasp

the landscape
that is offered

& has everything
to do with me,

& you,
even here—

this small pocket
of earth the moon

is already
reimagining

Ausschusskinder: the garbage children

*I gave the Berlin bear a solemn crown, but when your mother
town is estranged from you, death can't be far away.*
—Bruno S.

Your accordion transmits *orphanage*, the song
a field for the white horse

you dreamed as a child brutalized by Nazis.
In the video, bells with their brass patina

yoke together with string and pitch, your hand
a hummingbird over each

as you sing and squeeze
the wheezy box. Yet what of the song's

translation: *Mamatschi, give me a little horse.
A little horse would be my paradise.*

How the boy of the song becomes a man
when the horse that he prayed for

arrives years later pulling the hearse that bears
his dead mother. And what of the city

that swallowed its own? Discarded prayers
in mint-green walls of the psychiatric ward

where you cling to the others in a circle, trembling.
Years later, still trembling,

you watch the Berlin wall fold into itself
under the uncountable stars.

End of Blood Orange Blossoms

She throws white sheets like sails
over fruit trees, those pale
phantoms of the field.
The wide arc of her arm gestures
toward the entire lost fleet, sweeping

the March air, brittle
as bark. The season's frost
reaches the shore as branches

bend under her hand, their bright
wing-flutter of fabric
in this orchard by the sea. Ten years

since her son's body knocked
against the wide sandy belt.
His eyes were groundfall
fruit, overripe, his toes raised
their blue scalloped edge.

Her song: *Tomorrow they may keep.*
She blankets another tree, her fingers
dark as the marmalade she'll cook
tomorrow morning, syrupy

as a baby's tongue. Her arms
roll like waves, a bright flame of cloth

catches the moon. With every snap
of sheet, she feels
his fingers curled like thorny
leaves catching at her skirt,

then slipping from her hip
to settle like childhood over the coast.

Pause

December: even the fowls out back

     curse its arrival, everything branch-fractured

in hardened light, the pond's face

     gone matte with dead algae, a brisk wintriness

over each angle and plane, lavender shadows,

     a square of distorted window glass between you

and what is no longer possible.

     This is the moment you couldn't have foreseen

when four years ago your only child

     died, hours turned to nights, churning seasons,

and if it was last week it was two months

     since fall dropped her sherbet-colored skirts.

The lapse is a pause on the stair

     where you've forgotten from which direction

you've come. The needle and spool

     of thread in your hand says *how soon will this*

be over, though her yellow room

    calls you back, its solid surfaces, clothes hung

neatly in the closet, the growth chart that stays

    penciled on the doorframe ending with *June*.

Shadow and Act

—after Eugenio Montale

The plume's ocher tip invents
your face, as the sun's blade plays
hide-and-seek through stained glass
and returns it from a child's mirror.
Along the stone walls, a brown fog
pockets the poplars' church,
while below on the street
the butcher's parrot rearranges its feathers.
Then the sultry, lonesome night over the square,
over steps, and always the tired grind
of going down to come up again—
in a moment, a century—nightmares
that keep me from finding your eye's lit match
in a cave. Still the same howls,
the same weeping on the veranda.
If a shot fires—reddens your throat,
snaps your wings, O perilous messenger
of dawn—then its echoes sound reveille
waking cloisters and hospitals
to the shrieking of trumpets...

St. Maximos in the Blue Margin

Barefoot again   on the stony footpath
and muttering   below his breath.

I would give him a loaf for supper.

What lonesome   burning madness.

His walking stick won't order the dusk
or the apparitions   that must gather

at the rim   of sight.

I imagine angels
                with black tongues

spinning round his head.

Little hut burner, fire   in the ear.

Knife in the ear.
            And for what?

Every blue flame   a contemplation
deepening   its own suffering.

Little nest killer,   little here-we-go-again.

There is nothing I can do to save you.

No radiance of the heart   big enough
to keep sorrow   from catching

or your tongue   from being plucked out.

The hours   building crude huts

of brush and branches.   Each, in time,

he'll coax into a bud   of fire.

Devotion

I will imagine my child alone in a room of slaughtered
goats. I must think of her this way, worshipped
as a *kumari*. The Buddhist priest peers inside her
mouth, admires thirty-two perfect attributes,
her scarless birth chart, legs of a banyan tree—a body
to be inhabited by the spirit of Taleju. The hands
that have pinched the hair on the back of my neck,
offered the rouged meat of persimmon, are now
painted amaranth. If she withstands the trials,
she will be the next living goddess of Nepal.

But first, she must walk the raw fields of buffalo heads,
eye sockets lit with candles. Sip from a horse's
skull. All this she must do without fear, her calm
mistaken in the red, slow-pouring shadows.

Clematis

It slips into the night sky
behind her as the evening
slides into its black dress.

Her first dance:
her date will pick her up

at the family orchard where her mother,
unable to walk, peers
from an upstairs window, the sill thick

with strands of dead flies. Once,
she had looked just like her daughter—

the dress widening at the knees
as though emptied of all
thought, a single dented pearl

pulsing at her throat. The quiet held
in the tank house cobwebs spreads over

the valley that glistens under the moon's
snow-blue blades. If the girl
was surprised by his spent silhouette,

the blood-lacquered back seat,
it was the acreage of stillness,

the day continuing its drift
like the others with no memory
of its former self. The pinwheel

petals won't keep the world from going
gray and plump with hate on the vine.

Codex of the Andes

The machete's silver arc slices
                    a lone orchid hanging:
grandmother, the guide calls it—
                    a long chin-hair bright in sunlight's
yellow pour. Rock after rock,
                    dust, then more crushed
stone and water, steep cliffs
                    that sluice into liquid
that takes them down,
                    my feet strike it all—
a steady march of pounding
                    as it must have been
for the Inca who traveled
                    the packed earth for their god,
a *quipu*'s knot ordering the sun.
                    New rain and underbrush,
tangled bushes startle
                    our pace. Every stump or broken
twig, bone and insect shell,
                    each tree-limb bridge,
a condition of longing.
                    A scatter of horseshit
smells of rotted plums broken over
                    the white spine of Salcantay.
Here blood once reddened
                    a fragrant earth pocked
by footsteps of an open-
                    winged people whose ruins
now stand as gaunt witness—
                    portals to other worlds
underground, realm of the *apu*,
                    carved with a condor's beak.

Sirocco

The vineyard pitches over its cliff
toward the shale-gray sea. Sprayed
with ash and rust, each pumice hollow
spins down into itself like the spent caldera
at Santorini's core, yet the vines grow
tangled and strong as the vintner's daughter.

Every injury's a black fruit that turns,
like devotion, toward the sea. Long ago
he bathed her in a bucket of rainwater,
each drop wrung from the cloth into her mouth
light as the pulse beneath her skin and clear
as the hours of mineral dusk spent grafting
new branches to ancients 3,000 years old.

Each grain of sand is another open prayer.
What remains will test a long afternoon—
he prunes each vine into the shape
of a basket, a haven for clutches of grapes,
convinced he can train longing
like any tendril—take an aimless blank jumble
and alter it. Resisting his thirst as long
as he can, he will not stop until
every sallow globe is held safe. Even here

love tenses against disappointment.
When he's finished, sky folds
into its darkening silk. The donkey sleeps
against the shed. The daughter slips away
in a freshly laundered blue dress.

Rilke's Eighth Letter

i.

Creped by touch, dog-eared
& stained, yellowed

in the flimsy light, the words
of this letter may both hold you

in place & carry you
from *all that is*

to *all that might be.* They say
relax in suffering & exhale.

Liddy: your one bright comet,
your child, her last fatigued breath

spent, as depleted soil might feed
one crop, then another, and on

until the constellation
of sorrow that follows,

fathomless, is yet surprising
the ways it opens out

year after year.

ii.

The way it has always been:
        1996 in my hometown,

Old Lyme on the Connecticut coast,
      the silvered & damp cold

burrowing its head beneath
      every lining. I'm at a bar

with Charles, elbowing
      the after-work crowd,

buzzed with forgetting,
      crushed peanut shells

beneath our feet,
      the thread of the horizon

shimmering beyond
      a red neon sign.

What were our hopes
      that night he tickled

my palm with a halved nut
      below the table?

Each day they diminish,
      those spectral currents,

dissolved into woods now
      ghostly as his car,

or that following night,
      the slide across black ice,

its nose accordioned
      on the oak's splintered bone,

the vast quiet holding in its arms
       the one sound—Led Zeppelin,

"Ramble On," playing
       through the car's mangled

dash, insisting on its own arrival
       in that abiding stillness.

iii.

You ask if I'm forgetting,
or want to, if,
among the blurred city
lights, what opens
isn't so much acres
of night, but a small grace
placed in every room,
as your hand moves
in orbit over each page,
the way you circle
the house, searching
the empty windows.

THREE

Augury

Because bones are stamped with hours, sky.

Because bones are ice, wing, pearl.

Because we are tethered to the ground.

Because our daughters are harbingers of dusk.

Because the spine is chambered and ancestral.

Because bones weather and migrate to surface.

Because bones are mineral within the catacombs,

there is wind inside the bone.

The Golden Age of Herbalists

When he throws a fist of parsley into the pond,
        the man believes the ailing fish will heal. In 1540,

      William Turner studied plants for the resolve
          within each one: wolfberry for scars;
lye from gentian roots to clean cloth;
    cardamom to soothe snake venom.

As a boy, he had found his mother on the kitchen floor,
        body bent in half, coughing, eyes watering

      and locked on a distant plane. He fed her evening
primrose oil and the immense choke loosened;
      she breathed once again.

They were more than simples to heal bones
    and cure diseases—he studied their moods, their networks of
be seed, be influence. You, who are always trying.

      When he finally took to the countryside, he carried
      a sack and a knife, dusk settling

on leaf-points as if in the summer months
       their passions were precisely edged.
      Standing alone in the meadow, he knew everything

he caught sight of was in the dying
      and would die before he would, yet he held

        in his hands a garden, an herbal
he would pen against sickness, soreness, wounds,

the formulas behind the labyrinth of green
        unfolding before him.

A Theory of Emergence

In the dream, you whirr
a scythe above your head
scattering white birds
across a field who fly
their clouds until even
the sky no longer
remembers what
edge,   what difference.

      My bonfire,
my wick
and bleeding star,
brother—

the only tradition
in this place for miles,
whiskey's single malt
erasing frost in your eye,

hands that break   open
like pollen disassembled

tell me again
of bee economies—
the colony acquires
meaning over time
that transcends   its parts—

You were there once
in another life
before we each became
unmerciful as the moment
a lake absorbs
its mirror of sun

Before My Mother Set Herself on Fire

the house fragrant with shepherd's tea
attendant on the yellow fields near Volos
the dog leaping for joy upright on its hind legs
long hours in the kitchen my mother drew
an essence from rose petals until the house
the house became—what?

my father splintered as rain his frame
top-heavy hair still dark & full
haywire in the breeze before his heart
lost its way & the cane tricked him
into old age when the money was gone

my mother falling asleep in a soap opera
blaze poppies nodding in a jar
on the stove the house taking on
the stillness of snow the absent look
of snow coming into her gaze turning
the gray of unseeing & on the other side

of the room my father growing
inward & suspicious of every last ship
in the harbor whose lights burned furious
and cold as the ache inscribed
on the smoking waters beneath
the inked sweep of night's only cloud

Among the Maniots

For every cliff there's a caique,
unmoored, refusing the shore's

prim neckline. If I could write a letter
to every girl not yet born

in the Peloponnese of 1808,
I would tell how my brother

was made to sleep in the shed
with the lambs, a ruse to throw Charon

off the scent, and of pirated cowry shells,
those little wombs I stitched beneath

my bed so that I might not be taken.
Where a feud for arms and the fuel needed

for burning lime are nearer
than dreams, where here, in the Mani,

honey cakes are bitter, poppies spell suffering,
an egg mutters *vendettas are brewing*.

There are no dowries,
only boys, known as *guns*—

another gun for the family!
Girls are dirge-singers,

gun-breeders.
We are partial to the carved sun

at the head of a boy's cradle, the moon,
that pale palsied wrist, for the daughter

whose birth is a hardening
silhouette against the mountain.

Every wilderness of ache, every impulse
to sea arrives through the threadbare hours.

When the mirror was held above
my limp body, my immobile face,

no breath clouded the glass,
only a black sun of starlings

shone in the silver medallion tied
around my throat, the sky tender, kempt.

Letter to the Egyptian Fishmonger

—Rafina, Greece

Tables are tossed, mackerel scattered
like rats across the market floor. Stacked
ice melts around the wasp-black boots
of this cadre of Greece's Golden Dawn
while lyrics from Pogrom, the party's favored
band, pump them on: *Rock
for the Fatherland, no parasites,
no foreigners in our land!*
They've come in crash helmets,
waving flags painted with golden
meanders drawn like swastikas
to scrape the country clean.
Tonight, I'm writing you,
fishmonger, because in the video
they slap at your face with chains.
My mother would have called them
goons back when witness was genteel,
when polite society didn't speak
of such things—it's the willed, tense quiet,
the same awkward silence that met Yeats
when he spoke of belonging
to his own Golden Dawn
in the 19ᵗʰ century and their aim
to cleanse the soul through alchemy
and spirit travel. While I won't claim
a rinsed soul, I know that pain
is a mind that refuses a new face.
Tonight, there's no wind, no cloud—
only a presidential debate pirating
the airwaves. Now, in your hospital
room, bandaged with strips
of gauze, the woman at your side

may whisper of a paper moon,
tin-hearted stars. Maybe she, too,
no longer believes there's a country
mindful enough to hold you. I know
it hurts to hear of it, the night's burned
tongue wrapping itself around you.

Master of the Bonsai

Astonishing, the resistance
   of the smallest branch.

Having torn her shrimp-pink robe.

Having tied her thrashing arms
and gripped her throat, stilling

   her body, I made her *bonsai*,

   scenery—though now she returns

in the blood red leaf
   of a dwarf maple,

Count Okuma's favorite tree,

   points rigid as a girl's knees.

Unkind, unlike other leaves
   whose blades I've curled

down into a loose
   feathery cascade.

Though I've pinched the buds
   so the petals swoon

   in unison, though for years
     I've twisted stems, pruned roots

to please my lord, still your vagrant face stiffens
   in that defiant gesture

I've worked so hard to conceal

in uncounted winters of wire.

Letter to Tryfon Tolides

—Korifi Voiou, Greece

You might wish a little to be carried off.

   A silver cup in the cupboard

mirrors your mother's gray face, vacant

   as the bombed field around a village.

If a shrine is what you need to bring her back

   every day, who can blame you for trying?

If sleeping in her nightgown brings the scent

   of custard into your dreams, and running

barefoot in the snow seizes your body

   into memory, who among us can say

anything and not turn quietly away. Linens

   just as she left them pressed and folded.

A needle upright in a drift of stiff lace.

   What I know of your mother I know

of a bear, thieving and brown, we once searched

   for in the hills behind your house, followed

the newly-ripped branch until the path

   no longer parted and became even more itself.

Black laurel will do this under a lonesome moon.

Tonight there is frost on the ground—the earth

no longer able to muster the energy to care.

   Winter intends to neglect you.

The room in which she washed her feet

   means to lock you outside its heavy door.

There's nothing wrong with slipping

   through the house at night with her ring

tucked inside your mouth, the taste

   of metal the same copper as blood.

Even calling a stray dog *Filos* won't keep

   the black plums from rotting. It's easy to say

all this to you after whiskey, a hard-slung year.

   Easy to mistake the sound of an almond tossed

into a well for whatever follows weeping.

Retrograde to Desire

A heart blunt as stored pleasure—
          Ophelia floats on her back

in black water, eyes settling
          on a sparrow, the swath of

its head and delicate yellow thoat.
          Though half-dead, she's held

by flicks of wings and breaks of light
          behind. Below: water

is a spell, swallowing night.
          —a demon, a stranger

stealing through a window.
          Crows. The water calling

to water, the drink of silk,
          pansies at her fist. Liquid

petals from the necklace
          around her throat. A wind swifts

hair. A final feather's pendulum
          ticks the sky open, open, open.

Little Death

With the hooked curve
of a clavicle
stolen from the museum,
the end turned up *just so,*

small bones of her hand
working, her purpose is

to die by orgasm—*bone-wing*
of orchid, death
star shower, mulberry
drumfire—to make her own

ticker stop. She has made me
promise to have her ashes
heated and pressed
into a diamond,

cut and polished for the stud
I'll pierce through my clit.

Go on and say it, Hellbender.

I'll be your shock wave
of oxygen, your Andromeda.

Beehive and buttercup.

When my blood pills on the lip,
I'll withdraw the ache.

Everything I Wanted

He begged me to twist his nipples
into shocked scarlet berries,

keep the hazard of my mouth
locked shut. If my jaw moaned
open even once, he'd push it back

into place—into silence vast
as the hem of low country.

I'd do anything back then
for a line or a vodka shot,
demons climbing up like egrets

flying out of black water,
men with their hearts grabbing,
bodies pouring. The tenderness

of my breasts proof
I'd done everything I wanted

no real part of. The body at twenty
still new, dumb as the hitchhiker
whose sign reads *Wherever,*

who leaves behind his carnival
past and the one that came before.

You'll forgive my undressing,
its indiscriminate urge—lips
a kink, a refusal not to tell.

Notes

"Requiem Wind" is inspired by George Seferis's poem "The Thrush," translated by Edmund Keeley and Philip Sherrard.

"Shadow and Act" is a very free translation of Eugenio Montale's "Day and Night."

"Letter to Tryfon Tolides" begins with a first line from Sappho's fragment number 88, translated by Willis Barnstone.

—Jay Paul

Michele Poulos is an award-winning poet, screenwriter, and filmmaker. Her chapbook, *A Disturbance in the Air,* won the 2012 Slapering Hol Press competition, and her poetry has been anthologized in *Best New Poets 2012* (chosen by Matthew Dickman) as well as *The Southern Poetry Anthology.* She has published poetry and fiction in such journals as *The Southern Review, Smartish Pace, Crab Orchard Review, Sycamore Review,* and many others. Her essays and book reviews have been published in *Blackbird, 32 Poems,* and *Stone Canoe,* and her screenplay, *Mule Bone Blues,* won the 2010 Virginia Screenwriting Competition. She holds an MFA degree in poetry from Arizona State University, and an MFA in fiction from Virginia Commonwealth University; earlier, she earned a BFA in filmmaking at New York University's Tisch School of the Arts. Recently, she has produced and directed a feature-length documentary film titled *A Late Style of Fire* about the poet Larry Levis.

CPSIA information can be obtained
at www.ICGtesting.com
Printed in the USA
BVOW03s1821301017
499078BV00001B/35/P